MALAK

poems by JENNY
SADRE-ORAFAI

PLATYPUS PRESS, England

Copyright 2017 by Jenny Sadre-Orafai
All rights reserved.

ISBN 978-1-9997736-0-1

First Edition, 2017

Cover and interior layout by Peter Barnfather
Cover art: *Still Life with Game Birds*, by Pieter A. Wakkerdak
   – courtesy National Gallery of Art, Washington
Type set in Bergamo Pro, FontSite Inc.

Printed and bound by Clays Ltd, St Ives plc

Published by Platypus Press

for Haj Khanoom

for Nate and for Bella

I

3 Burning in a Hot Moon
4 Mouthing the Future
5 Chirology
6 Forecasting
7 How They Arrive
8 Path to the Split-Log Home
10 Lots, Enormous Spaces
11 Hearing Secrets
12 Autobiography at Fifty Feet
13 Company
14 Wearing It Out
15 Last Reading
16 Queen of Cups
17 Karaj
18 You Will Meet a Man
19 Call and Response
20 A Break and a Fracture

II

25 Origin

III

- 37 When I'm Just Dead
- 38 We Can't Change the Orbits Quite Yet
- 40 Lucy Let People See
- 41 Markers
- 42 Frequency Interference
- 43 Toll Road
- 44 Round Lake Yearbook
- 46 We Buried the Fathers in Northville
- 47 Listen
- 48 Mother Spell
- 49 Jamshid's Angoor
- 50 I Saw You'd Be Born
- 51 Gospel
- 52 Piloting
- 53 Lifecasting
- 54 Language of Signs
- 56 Blank Nature

- 63 Acknowledgements
- 65 About the Author

I

Burning in a Hot Moon

*I was born to a dying moon, a dead room. You were born
to a hot moon, a burnt view.* What moons do

before we're alive is up to them. This moon is seven days
old. Malak draws a house on a house wall. *Here's you,*

your room, crickets for luck—jumping in your closet. I draw fire
on windows. I swallow the air and down each kite.

Mouthing the Future

My father tells me not to tell my friends.
They won't believe how your grandmother sees

patterns divide, gold fields in coffee, a foxtail
twitching in the seam where the handle

meets the cup. I believe so hard that I write
down her language of residue. I ask, *Who*

will tell us what happens after she's gone?
Don't put that future in my mouth—I can't say it.

Chirology

When we sent you out for fire,
you always returned with ash.
White palm bones flooding
black film, we thought you'd see
the rind, the shine your body makes.
We thought you must have changed
your path, disrupted lines to a future
now gone ghost. We thought you must
have seen yourself being robbed,
of the first and second wives, both
brunette, of twin and identical boys
with their mother's eyes, of the house
with two chimneys and five identical doors,
then, of that terrific sun that comes before
the house is blown apart by storm.

Forecasting

Gulps of grey crown
an exhausted sky.
On the other side
we are safe, away with
crickets who sing
without pause. To see
a storm approach
someone and not call
is pulling a ladder away,
is readying your ears
for the blast.

How They Arrive

They carry cups like newborns to her,
careful with all their hope.

She points at coffee grounds:
bags of money in houses

and mouths filled with straight teeth.
A peasant woman who couldn't read

taught Malak how when she was young,
when she didn't know how much people

needed to be told what was coming.
A snake with its jaw-hinge slack.

Path to the Split-Log Home

Our cloudbursts sing,
most are welcome!

Our planting is dictated
by the zodiac.

Our trapdoors lead
to sweet potatoes.

Our earth is wild—
horseradish, boneset, peppermint.

Our baby girls and boys
wear dresses.

Our mothers step on infant hems,
keep them from harm.

Our trees can only be killed
after we cut rings around them.

Our first frost means
now we kill the hogs.

Our sheep distrust
wanderers in pants.

Our snakes won't die
until sundown.

The sisters ask that you leave
the same door you entered.

Lots, Enormous Spaces

She's translating what hasn't happened yet.
She isn't inventing it. I can't speak

her language, so her son translates
the translation. Even when

she's speaking the present it sounds like
she's talking the future.

She uses her free hand to tell me: *lots
of weddings* or *lots of money* or *I will meet*

*the short man who will buy me lots
of presents*. Always lots of everything.

Lots, enormous spaces, where gloom is
waiting for her to turn the cup back over.

Hearing Secrets

Hold the beginning in a hand.
Remove what's missing,

vowels that will save you.
Broken emblems are gestures

on faces posing for love or food or money.
Lean away from what you remember.

Nod until a twin life lands
in another hand.

Autobiography at Fifty Feet

We'll write our autobiography when we're teenagers,
before we grow into our teeth. Before we meet
people who will laugh at us for reasons we'll talk about
when we're older and divorced. And we'll both still know
our exes because we have to, not because we want to.
We'll write our autobiography just before we kiss
in the log flume tunnel, our log smacking against the rail,
and we'll pretend, for that part of the ride, we are old and blind.
We'll write that I squirmed next to you when you said
there were snakes and that they'd launch themselves
like canned confetti into our log, that wasn't really a log
of course, that the kids, somewhere behind us, said
the water smelled like urine. We'll tell everyone
in our autobiography that our teeth glowed
in that darkness when we laughed.

Company

Malak hears futures in cups the way we
hear oceans inside shells. Families we know rush
through Turkish coffee, scalding their throats.
They wear black stripes down their tongues like
Plains garter snakes, leave enough to
drip when propped against the saucer. We exchange
the quiet of living rooms, waiting until the inside
dries, until it stops drawing.

Wearing It Out

The other grandmother wore a shot fox across her shoulders.
I pet its paws when she visits the grocery store.

There were so many looks. The fox's eyes, stuck open,
looking back. Children tugged parents in aisles.

A sleeper bag hung, waiting for it to return. I thought
at least the fox has its own room, and its own eyes.

I'd knock and ask it to play. I don't know why she took it out
so much, all that dying waiting to take her.

Last Reading

There is a pregnant bird in the cup.
Malak looks at me like she has never looked

at that in a cup before. My father looks at me
like there are things I'm not telling him.

She crochets baby caps, square blankets,
booties in Neapolitan ice cream colors.

If I ever have these babies, if I'm the bird
in the cup, I'll want to devour them.

After the last reading, she leaves the cup turned up,
daring the bird to forget I was pregnant.

Queen of Cups

Queen Elizabeth was with Philip in Kenya
when her father died. She was watching

elephants from a hotel within the trees.
My father was with his three sisters when

his mother died. I was with my bed,
hallucinating a fox. After the fox left,

I called him, but he was taking a shower.
Like a movie, the protagonist crying

surrounded by water, lots of empty cups?
Was Elizabeth instructed not to cry?

It will shake this tree.
The elephants will trample this nest.

Karaj

When I miss her, I open my popout map. Spilling my face
into Tehran streets, I hide in Laleh Park. Read street names
aloud like I'm reporting to someone. I pretend to see things
no one else can—who took the Peacock Throne, how
the burnt city fell. I say *Karaj* like I'm telling the future.

You Will Meet a Man

I stood on him,
a well of dirt
that mends,

and breathed in
his boyhood,
what's left of air

in altitude.

I could recite
every line on his hand,
behind his ears.

Should I tell it—

we will live
against the knife.
Your mother,

a girl,
watched sharpen,
wane, and then

a flat line.

Call and Response

Nine ladders is the dream that keeps
coming—its back with kites, all diamonds,

between the rungs. The ninth dream
is nine ladders with bows at their necks,

diamonds in their ears and violet sandals
climbing every rung. Nine times the nine ladders

that go nowhere, no back to waking up
in cups that can't speak.

A Break and a Fracture

Break

The sun falling made the bone yellow then pink
then black. I left it there. Had I brought it to her,

she would touch my tooth whole, cover the empty
space in a girl's mouth.

Fracture

I fell down concrete stairs, landed on elbow or wing.
Her son's hands and working elbows fastened hair away

from my face, his daughter, each morning. *Have you
seen the sad film she's left over us?*

Have you watched bone knit itself together like the future?

II

Origin

I made the door lock without a key, once without a hand. I like to think it came from Malak and not the woman at the co-op. My grandmother and I wore the same shoe size, wore the same small bird shoulders too. The woman at the store says, *we looked alike when I was younger*. Her hair looks like it's been bleached in a bathroom, and cut there, too. I nod when she tells me, *you're like my twin*. Nodding is the polite thing to do when we have different color eyes.

If I concentrate hard on something, I can make it happen —car glass shattering, radios shutting down, computers going dark. I've never known an actual lumberjack, but I wrote the word lumberjack once. Twice now. I didn't tell anyone—I went to school the next day. In my classroom, a fortune left from someone's cookie. In red: *The lumberjack must always keep a sharp ax*. I carried the paper with me until it wasn't there anymore.

I dated a man who wore a spear through his ear cartilage, helix to lobe. It flashed when he told me not to be afraid of everything that blinked around me. *It's reassurance that you are exactly where you should be.* He explained numbers and Japanese superstitions and things I can't recall because they no longer matter.

I like looking at pictures of identical twins or I like pretending that someone's given me two pictures and I have to spot the differences. I look at Malak sometimes like she's my twin or I search her face for the pieces I can't see in mine.

I locked the bedroom door without realizing. I felt like I was in a cave and I needed him to throw more light than he could. We painted the outside of the house in neons, like the eighties. I didn't swell into the room fast enough. There was no husband to shine my way out. My hands didn't turn the lock.

I cannot tell you how to walk on agony, on defeat. Oh, there's no trouble in this song. Why shouldn't we be brave in the light of everything flashing? Drop your walk. Run in every road. Forget sleeping for weeks. Today, I tried to wipe a crumb from my pants but it was the sun.

My other grandmother was kept on a farm and tried to convince the circus to take her. At night her daddy came for her, followed exotic animal noises in the fields. Maybe she had magic in her own green eyes. I never saw it. She wasn't magic like Malak, with the bird shoulders and hands that were wrinkled even when she was young.

Raw quartz is rock candy disguised as broken caves, makes me sleep like I can't stop. I take every amethyst and trade it for rubies. They don't bring sleep. Their red is loud and her favorite. I pack them into the pillowcase. She'll come back for the nest.

The right rear tire of the car in front will burst. Both hands on the wheel like my father taught me in a high school parking lot, like all fathers. I won't move from the tire's path. I'm daring it to do what I tell it. Several minutes later, the tire blows. I know and I swerve.

III

When I'm Just Dead

I'll send a fox to my daughter. It will nest in her hair,
my heaviest sleeping girl—largest heart outside my body.

She will shove it aside, look for me in a tin box
of necklaces I circled her with when she was a cricket.

She'll drink water from a bottle too tight at the lip.
She'll draw my face on the wall and tell it everything.

We Can't Change the Orbits Quite Yet

We have long talks about
what color my blood really is,

how many hearts the octopus can
make breath and still swim with.

I think the Hudson is the river
and not the dog. I want the shoulder

and muscles, the muzzle to be a rounded
wave. We can make it make sense.

Here's the octopus, eight hearts
beating within each tentacle.

Here's my open finger
and my black blood.

Here's a man walking his pressed shirt
down the rainy street anyway.

Here's the muscle in his jaw moving
up and down, a seesaw.

Here's his shoulder pushing
out of your wave and into

a message from my mother
in pictures. She's past words

now and I hear every thing
she means. The sound

of a small plane in the suburban
sky is my father saying hello.

Lucy Let People See

I'm alone in the back of a cab.
The driver is telling me about the Awash
and Lucy's bones. He talks of them
like I talk of futures. *Lucy let people see.*
His hands are the longest I've ever seen.
I think of what his skeleton must look like,
languid and slippery. We talk about languages
we know, how many other ways we could be
having this conversation. He takes me through
a tunnel that reminds me of a cave, a depression.

Markers

First coyote

First big rock

First pink sky

First bruise

First fork

First well water

First cricket

First spell

First fast

First shadow

First villain

First fire

First no

Frequency Interference

My ears ring when an airplane's
in the next town.

Call it frequency. Call it
magic. Invisible headphones
with singing bells.

Should I push my wings
out too? Carry the crying
babies behind my teeth?

It's true that Malak's a white plane
on a white cloud, reading
land, laughing
at winking rivers,
waiting for me to turn

gold, gold, gold, gold.

Toll Road

I learn two words in sign language.
Heaven and *Heel.* They are side by side.

If I run into the fox again, I'll tell her heel,
like you tell a tame animal.

I will tell her where to put the grandmother
she took. And I will keep a look out.

Round Lake Yearbook

The way you know today is by getting mad
at the stars, the chickens, the lists,
at the noisemakers mostly.

The way you know what time it is
is by reading glow-in-the-dark stickers
on an overhead fan that belonged to your teenage self.

The way you predict the future and don't tell anyone
is the same way you know you will ruin every manicure
on purpose by eating pistachios.

The way you carefully pass a school bus
with a sign across the back: DRIVER IN TRAINING.
The way the phrase fits the situation.

The way we don't have to be this loud when we're old.
Our bones are good news. They heal on their own.
Our bones are the best things to keep us standing.

The way, when I mentioned your name, all the rabbits
and hares came out of the forest and smelled
a different air, their whiskers trembling.

The way your hairline falls into my face
and every dream happens again but on different roads,
and you put me in my grave and you see it.

The way other people I can't think of right now
don't make us sisters with so many dreams,
with so many windows open or let down.

The way we handle the life and death of public art.
The way we tell the mural good news,
bad news, how it is still in need of urgent care.

The way that man who lived five miles away
was a gunman, how we gave money
for their funerals in Wisconsin.

The way we tell the cicadas to please hit more notes.
The way the new finch doesn't know space.
The way we fall into place around Round Lake.

The way no one here is awake yet.
The way we raise the dead is real.
Our whole gold life is happening.

We Buried the Fathers in Northville

Air pours out of a defeated tire on the highway.
We point. We say *ghost*. There goes the rim
sparking, a firecracker.

And when we see the windmill next
to the barn on some small road,
we say, *Michigan, you don't know how to look*

real. Your trees are stretched gold coins
pulled from a top hat.
You make our mouths miss the dead.

We know somebody's dad will walk out
to the square with its bumpy sidewalks,
shake his pockets clean for pebbles, push them

inside his leather shoes. He will suffer
for our suffering as long as it hurts. Surely,
we can still the windmill if we want harder.

Listen

We found the first bird behind the museum near Sixteenth.
We held hands and it wasn't vulgar until we were standing

at a funeral. Yes, I let go first. My wings pulled in tight.
Death is the most comfortable suit.

And I wanted to take its picture like the bird was going off
to its first day of school.

I wanted to pick it up, put it in the front seat, drive it
back home. I wanted you to say something.

The second bird sounded like a baseball hitting
my bedroom window, somebody's best arm pitching.

But it was a flat cloud of oil and down. Listen, that's two.
Their song is here and I can't put it back into their mouths.

It's autumn, and it's in the trees that look like fire.
The birds listen, even after dark.

Mother Spell

I felt for mountain
and ocean, my first globe.

Mouth or beak. Arm or wing.
Skin or feather. Feet or feet.

Who brought these to me
to dress in booties and caps.

I didn't ask to know a belly
so tight.

I didn't ask if it was girl
or boy or bird.

Jamshid's Angoor

In the spring I am at my childhood home.
My father goes to and from the store
with dark grapes for his daughter.

He holds them by the tops
of their heads to the sink, drops
them in a bowl. Dunking them,

he pulls them out like he's making
something more than grapes clean.
He's cautious with his hands like

he's a father of an infant again.
Like he's a father of an infant again
who makes her body go corpse

every time she hits water and then
waits for the attention, the calling,
the bringing of her body back to life.

I Saw You'd Be Born

A rainbow shadow
lapping around you,
you'd take time
with nature. I saw
your teeth come
crooked, canine,
you wouldn't bite
before you were bit.

Gospel

You're still running from the chain
letter you didn't write because you saw

your life would be safe, miraculous,
your apartment filled with balloons

bobbing, shoving their way into ceilings
and, if only, the sky. The person you love

most doesn't live with you but loves you
more than her hair that has its own way

into your undying succulent farm. So still
with your trunk, your arms, your legs when

you lie down because the streamers in
the blow of the heat are telling you

something you don't know yet,
and you call it truth.

Piloting

Draw a bath into the pit of a hand.
Tell the rabbit to drink there. Give

its heart slowness. What's left to scare
from. Wash its face, its thrumming

feet lucky. Open your mouth, carry
it to the next place, out of past,

present. Say, *here's your deepest sleep*.

Lifecasting

I stood for it, and the plaster felt
like the raw egg we wore on our tight,

tight pores. (We slipped the yellows,
full suns, down the sink.)

He demolded me after I read him
his hand. I said, *pick one*, from the pile

of parts. He pulled my other head, blank.
My other body, an empty piñata,

held up a wall. His hand over that
mouth means nothing.

Language of Signs

I slept the whole day
without remembering, Malak.

I dreamt I had a son
growing so fast,

a tomato plant sprawled
everywhere, unstoppable.

I held him at my hipline.
And I fed his hunger.

Now he's a pitcher
of water.

His teeth hiding
behind his father's lips,

or proud outside
of his mouth, like mine.

Then, Malak, I saw a nun,
a black veil trailed her head.

And I followed her like a ghost,
or bride.

Who has my voice?
Let me follow it.

Blank Nature

Dents in a window pause
at thunder and cross this
quiet horse. Draw him afraid
of an audience or that
best stable overrun with
hay and bridles and carrots
and tails swaying to what.
Then let him graze.

***

I don't have to tell you
that uncooked yolks
in the sunlight always
cancel each other out.
Practice scale. Now
suffering. Finally, heal.

You must drive a machine
to freedom. Its purpose
dissolves under foot.
Take back the factories,
I say. Rush into them
and rescue the workers.

***

Conduct a wetless
seashore, no more
suffering. No more
tight water. We aren't
up to our necks
in the charge.

You are a coat on water,
your own exhibit.

Your rabbit-heart is a prayer.

Blank nature is something
to steal, how you know fear.

    ***

Electric, you are the certain
vice, the important hands
that will invite the talking.

Your daughter is
your daughter because
she calls you
mother deer.

    ***

A blank picture
of a fire burning
is just broken bones.

A blank sound
when your daughter sees
a chick hatch from an egg
for the first time, her open
mouth cried
nothing.

**

A blank body
when somebody
grabs at your coat again.
You reach for the wool hem,
this belongs to me.

Acknowledgements

Thank you always to my parents, Stephanie, Nate, and Bella. I want to thank Michelle and Peter for all of their generosity, for the incredible editing and design, and for how wonderfully they care for their writers and their books. Thank you to Komal Patel Mathew for all of it. Rebecca Cook, thank you for pushing me to write when I don't want to and when I don't believe that I can. Heaps of love to Jennifer K. Sweeney for the keenest eye and biggest heart. I am beyond grateful to Airea D. Matthews and Wendy C. Ortiz for their brilliance and kindness. Thank you to my teachers—Earl Braggs, Richard Jackson, Beth Gylys, and Leon Stokesbury. Thank you Katherine Hyon, Kendall Klym, Aaron Levy, Bill Rice, and Sheila Smith McKoy for listening and reading. Thank you to the magic of Anne Champion, Susan Hankla, Joan Houlihan, Robin Shawland, Samantha Ten Eyck, Laura Watson, and Vanessa Zimmer-Powell at Colrain.

***

I am grateful to the editors and publishers of the following journals in which poems and prose in this manuscript were first published, sometimes in different versions: *The Bakery*, *The Collapsar*, *Dialogist*, *Los Angeles Review*, *MiPoesias*, *Mount Hope*, *Ninth Letter*, *PANK*, *Poemeleon*, *Redivider*, *RHINO*, *Tammy*, and *Thrush Poetry Journal*.

About the Author

Jenny Sadre-Orafai is the author of *Paper, Cotton, Leather* and five chapbooks. Her poetry has appeared in *Cream City Review*, *Ninth Letter*, *The Cortland Review*, *Hotel Amerika*, *The Pinch*, and other journals. Her prose has appeared in *Los Angeles Review*, *The Rumpus*, *South Loop Review*, *Fourteen Hills*, *The Collagist*, and other journals. She is co-founding editor of *Josephine Quarterly* and an Associate Professor of English at Kennesaw State University.

Please check the Platypus Press website for further releases.

platypuspress.co.uk